"The fates are wild, for they will; and the Almighty is wild above all, as fate is."

*Library of Coggins*

copyright
2022

published by
Gentle Blue Productions

All rights reserved

# *Foreword*

 W.A. Coggins has been writing since fourteen.
Drawn to music, he focused on songwriting, stashing
the poems in his desk drawer, sending to family and friends.
W.A. confides all these poems would "rise and converge."
That day has arrived with From The Bottom Drawer,
a compilation of Coggins "light side" he says with a grin.
His first book yields a happy yearning, the hopeful ending.

 Coggins' journey thru the drawer touches fifty years of writing.
The reader will find his Thoreau-like passion for the natural
elements. Rivers and twilight, necessities in his world.

 A relaxed, playful read, Bottom Drawer is a logophile must.
I invite you to follow William's quest for the perfect words to reveal his "grail," logical or mythological. Coggins' over-caffeinated,
colorful view of life believes one can find happiness anywhere, that
we are always in school – every day a lesson, a course in language,
a degree in time travel.

 Enjoy the trip.

To Mom and Dad.
For my wife and kids, their wives,
my brothers, their wives and children.

May every leaf on every family tree
feel love, know peace, savor life.

"Nor do we merely feel these essences
For one short hour; no, even as the trees
That whisper around a temple become soon
Dear as the temple's self, so does the moon,
The passion poesy, glories infinite,
Haunt us till they become a cheering light
Unto our souls, and bound to us so fast,
That, whether there be shine, or gloom o'ercast,
They always must be with us, or we die."

John Keats

# From
# The Bottom Drawer

the peripheries...

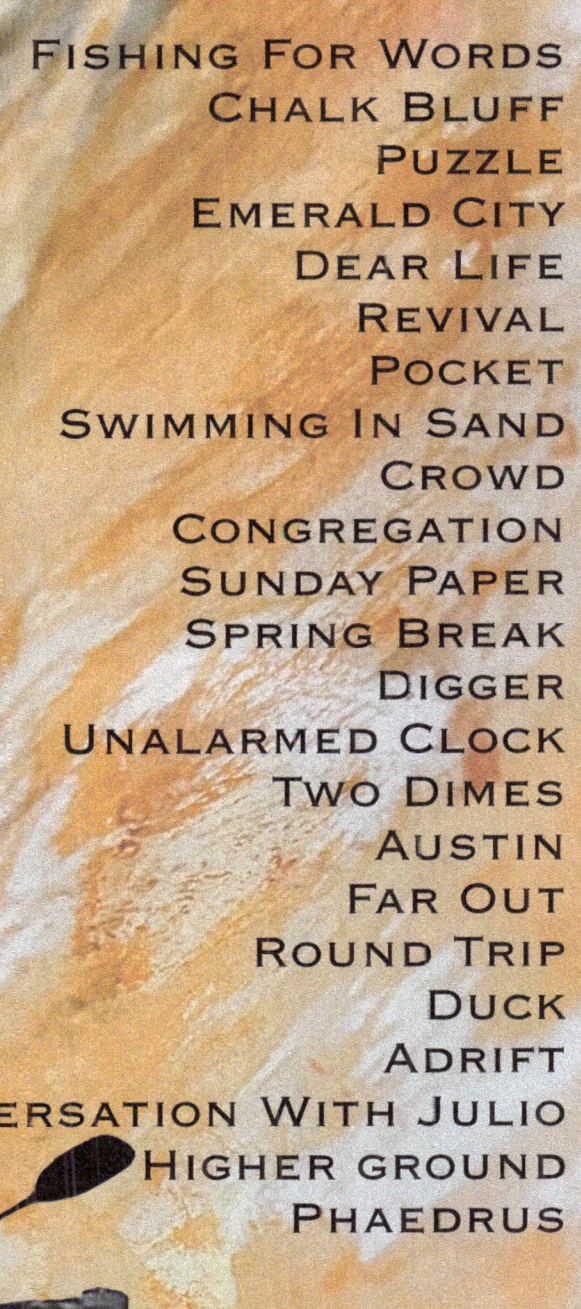

Fishing For Words
Chalk Bluff
Puzzle
Emerald City
Dear Life
Revival
Pocket
Swimming In Sand
Crowd
Congregation
Sunday Paper
Spring Break
Digger
Unalarmed Clock
Two Dimes
Austin
Far Out
Round Trip
Duck
Adrift
Conversation With Julio
Higher Ground
Phaedrus

## Fishing For Words

Solitude wanders
intimate streams
infinite windows
framed between
earthen walls
holding creeks
running away.
A river speaks.

Fishy words
slide by, fresh and lively
scaly schools of adjectives,
adverbs doing time: lifelong sentences.
All is created.

Single hook, patient
table for one.
Tasty dangles
respectful angles
the teeth of twilight,
the apex of a happy man's
blues.

Essence emanates, nourishes
a cathartic thesaurus:
full and sustained,
howling inside.

## Chalk Bluff

Lizard kings, backpacks creeping
caught the rest of us amphibians,
various forms of sleep.
Octaves of goodnight,
nocturnal sounds,
mammals in the night
draw the blinds.
Morning takes the long way.

Eyelids open stiffly -
no inner net,
"goofin' with the bees"
speaking with friendly hardheads,
small mouth families.
Dolittle would be proud.

>

Light chases
shadows down the bluff.
Heaven is not cloudy
today.
Cold and rowdy water
sometimes costly, calls out the play -
"Flow like a river
in and out tiny caves.
On two, break!"

A local knows where to dive,
backflips off the rope swing,
pushes the rope to outstretched hands.
He gets out fast then slips back in.
The turtles are pleased.
They know the name,
every mossy rock.

Around the bend, Blue Hole.
The kings relive their teens, Olympic dives
their place on the podium,
the illustrious, invisible record book.
Gold medal presence sees beauty, never perfection
in everything.

## Puzzle

Shadow Creator replies
Sky stands tall.
"Horizon sure *is* grinning about something."
Rain tickles rainbow's end -
cloud oblivion.

I pull over
some sunshine
thumbing a ride, disappears
after we stop for a bite.
She'll find another shadow
tomorrow.

Now is right.
Weather knows
morning, smug in its place
Downpour's a stone
thrown away…

Yonder shakes
actors up the holler,
midnight plays, Mission Drive In,
San Pedro Outdoor Theatre -
windows speaking.

Flurry carries me home, Dazy,
the eighth dwarf.
Crescent Moon hooks my casement.
Stars style a bedtime story,
the last piece snug
in today's jigsaw.

Emerald City

Woken,
wrong side of storm
dreaming of Dorothy,
Elton John.
Someone's always dreaming
when Morpheus comes round.


Boyish devils shoot crooked arrows.
Hypocrites change, genius rearranges.
Let the innocence remain,
the guilty become sane,
horses die lame,
fields of Monet.

In mountain scenes, writers conceive
language is a ring on a finger.
Canyon extends its hand, greets their words,
tongue is the poets' companion.

The yellow brick road feels the heat,
world we know is boiling.
*Little Drops of Rain* wake us, second winds
towards Emerald City,
déjà vu running thru
the pretty, pretty poppies.

## Dear Life

Kid, Camaro
running in place,
future's not approaching
his lingering chase.
Whispers to clues -
sirens, strange noises
precise steps
heels of damp tread.
Memories inch closer.

Work and play
teeter and totter. Dear life
wrings love, reeks
of money.  Callous hands tug
ropey rungs,
silver linings, the luster cluster:
Cloud 9.
Daunting jousts, glassy mounts.

>

Angels and demes
skate between
diamond dreams,
jellybeans.
A luminant future winks.


Kid polishes until they shine,
jewels, by hand, one at a time,
as many gems as he can find
inside the bright
game of twilight
crawling like a soldier.


Highway shoes, prints from racoons,
stream washes over a mirror, forgotten
time gone by.
Beauty can be a beast. And vice-versa.

At the least, truth speaks
even - against all odds.

Revival

Morning's ticked, pissed as it were,
pre-dawn pelt,
tin roof drips
squeeze the porch.
Windows scream.

Tolerance stares,
blank canvas sweeps
welcome mat dreams,
black and white summons
full color.
Truth lives in the mirror,
reflects Thor's departure.

Low rumbles grumble away
slow nimbus charcoal train.

City of rebirth
uncovers life and death,
communities
fat and lean,
fresh and clean
wet forest green:
smaragdine.

## Pocket

Slippers shuffle, drumming brushes
swish the narrow hall.
Eyes saunter, spy familiar
kitchen counter sees it all.
Bits of daybreak bellyflop
off the soap dish, punctuate stone tile.
I sweep up the shiny nuggets and put them in my
pocket.

While sunrise changes
guitar strings, syncopated
leaves cascade,
floating fingers, piano keys.
Couple notes cling to my PJ's.

Crispy piles, crunchy leaves -
oldest one rakes, waits to leap.
Two of the kids come in, wrestle and wear
themselves out. Brothers,
five and two.

Gathering them up to bed,
tokens of their day fall out of their pockets.
I place the keepsakes on their dressers.
A memory slips to the carpet.
I pick it up and place it in my pocket.

## Swimming In Sand

Egg-tooth first, wiggle second
tiny turtle legs
sand and species re-emerging,
tread trudge and trade
muggy dunes for submarine homes.
Their brave race for survival
counts toes, sticky wet stranded,
southeast zephyrs shrinking dunes,
the absence of predatory loons,
aquatic baboons.

Dozens of chelonians chase the gleam.
Though death may dwell forever,
death never enters the scheme.
The miniatures have little time
to rehearse their marching song,
waterproof papers in tow, many sing
muddy water blues.
Lucky and skilled hatchlings
make the wake,
snatch bubbles to the murky Gulf,
their holy home.

Crowd

Out of the car we hop
over the curb to stand
one-legged, flamingos,
back-lit mural.
Cleaved, locals stare at us,
neon pink.

Grocery cart carries some clothes, a variety
beer, smokes, a baby sleeping,
tattooed quilt.
We watch the young dad and mom -
lifelines circle the cart
full of silent understanding
hugs of the homeless.

No wind around the corner,
they back in and bundle.
We leave our blanket and picnic lunches
behind for another city,
princes and harlequins
playing beach volleyball.
We sub in, set-up and kill,
waking up in The Flatirons.


I like to run far away
always moving finds my way
out any place without enough space
extend my arms, spin around
fly all night upside down
with room for the sun
and landing gear.

## Congregation

Hobo-less freight train
cloud-breathing steel
tracks rail by
one room school.
Empty boxcars roll:
shadow, light
shadow, light -
quick rows of wheat
lick a thick field.
Church bells are heard
ahead of their time behind me,
the belfry above the stain.


Forefathers' hands clasp,
grab overalls next-door,
grandmothers gasp, grasp
bibles of faith, sing
gospels of grace, lighten the load,
tighten the belt.
Every prayer kneels.
Every sign begs
PRAY FOR RAIN.

Great aunts sing
hardy songs for children
aged by agile land.
Droughts are sad.  Sky, inactive.
Valley voices, *seco* souls, Indian shadows
scale the mountains, sandstone
mirages of a thermal sun,
eternal ripples of infernal thirst.

## Sunday Paper

Dad read the news every day.
I remember the sound the paper made
first time I stayed
up all night and hit the ceiling
when the newspaper cracked the sidewalk

above the fold of the middle
where the good Colonel thrived
on the Northeast side,
a creased life -
the pop of the page
precise.

I walk my friends, still chuckling,
halfway home, red right returning.
I take the hefty edition in.

I skim the front page,
take the frenetic news
still, never still enough.
Position the paper back in its bag,
sleep with the funnies.

## Spring Break

Sense, nonsense
the opposite view
nothing to do.
We power thru
something silly.
Summer dresses
differently.
Atman awakes, unclad.
Pillows dot eyes above,
pop-up canopies cross their "t's."

Pelicans cruise the coastline,
seagulls hover chips,
surfers stalk the waves,
beach boys shake some hips.

College student slowly strays
imaginary net along the quay.
Shares his prayer with the surf:
"If I can find just one unbroken one, I'll, I'll…"
New wave crashes in.
Shore reverberates "Keep perspective."


Labor brings us here, brought us here,
pays the way; we pay every day.
Countless hours, sweat and toil
minutes of powerful play
make the wallet open its heart -
front row to an imminent place.

## Digger

Music drives,
DJ pitches
daybreak off the walk,
local news on the side.
Path juggles coffee,
45-mile commutes,
five-hour wavelengths,
shoulders rub the morning.

Creation grows wild.
Wonderland glows
snow grows
blaze of cold
crocus crowing.
The Dead take wing.
Distant thunder coughs again.
I contemplate being
an older man.
Some clouds part.

Fate paid forward by Aeolus
purrs in *The Wind*.
Living is not a sin
for the strong.

Drive is over; he walks in grinnin',
diggin' everything he knows.
It's 6am.

## Unalarmed Clock

Surgeons open and close, 24/7.
Reverence prescribes on-call duty,
best and worst situations.
Hearts scar, stitches heal.
Organs untangle.


Barges browse
gulf, mesmerized
purviews. (The Earth is a child.)
Waxy moon wanes,
conscious of the slow turning,
whispers to the sun
softly applauding.

Sunsets warm hearts.
Stints of the day, tamped
perfectly, proud sundown.
Evening workers fetch nightfall, hoping
job loads to their liking.

Second shift yields, graveyard.
Workload gets tricky.
Silence surrounds the machines
hum; parking lot light's shot.
Embraced night waits -
sanguine sunrise.

Auburn orb sits on its iridescent throne
energizing whatever side
"You're on!"
Ready or not.

## Two Dimes

Twenty cents hit or miss
the lips you kiss when you kiss the lips
your man or miss.

Love is cool, fiery ice
dancing behind melting eyes,
emotional, aesthetic, security hangs
a key on a chain. On its desk lies
mystery, imagination - the screenplay.

Clues chase a devil, rusty war wagon rattles
needle half empty, splits tomorrow
with today, garbling
"The world is lusty."
Evidence comes between self
and actualization.

Vampires met, fixed cracks in the head,
inventoried hand baskets dictate
stakes pulled out too high, a lifetime to put back in.

Rezoned polar bear zigzags
white shadow in snow,
signs of a block party
not breaking apart,
*The Pilgrim's Progress.*
Will convenience, ever the art form, stop?
Rain forests cry.

Worth four nickels hit or miss
the target of common or uncommon sense.
Thin shiny coins, one jukebox kiss:
comedy and drama, paradigms shift.

## Austin 1980

Capitol City bounces
like Tigger
and one or two rent checks.
Shuttle, eggrolls, hot mustard, coffee
drag across the street,
the mulling green.  Deadheads meet
couple Shiners, The Hole in the Wall
snag a ride to Barton Springs,
join the soused, drenched throng.

The rising of the sun would never come.

Four kittens
church doorway, 6$^{th}$ street,
florescent eyes, calico feet,
unicycle juggles,
one-legged man peddles
red roses on the street.
Afternoon's tattoo stretches.
Tomorrow's rose could be white or pink.

>

Sunset full.
(Death is empty.)
Life gives its share
fair, unfair.
Cool evening, humid.
Spring smells of honey.
Red-tailed hawk.
Chipmunks stay in their burrow.
Stacy Park.

The rising of the sun is right around the corner.

Milto's wrappers grace the den.
Old couch blankets *Zen
and The Art of Motorcycle Maintenance*
napping.
Red and gold splinter
the horizon; orange peels
the morning sky,
yet to be reckoned with.

## Far Out

Kingfish fathom copper green
karate chops, thirty-pound degrees.
Fingertips thread
monofilament schemes, crew carries buckets
half full of dreams
and bait fish.


Sky introduces Jasmine to Lavender.
Experienced hands captain liquid sky -
Sea Ray smile slices swells,
navigates the JFK Causeway -
slow compass, steady ambit.
Throttle bounces whitecaps'
salty spray all the way, Baffin Bay
skyline waking, eyes fixed.


Optimism sinks
ambitious lines
food thinks
many meters meet,
preoccupied sea.


Anglers mine silver
holy mackerel miracles.
The golden hour bows.
Time bends.

## Round Trip

Plane is taxiing, pilot's not on it.
Heads in cumulus sky
look to the ground,
clouds chitter-chatter
what shape might *I* be
running down the flightline
yelling out a name.

The lawyer pleases the court,
stops the hourglass sift -
life for the madman
follows the bailiff,
mystery of why
a man can make everywhere
nowhere.

Nirvanic spells
half-light, daylight
wanes. REM finds the phone,
dream went on the wrong date.
Pilot awakes,
cold water to the face.

## Duck

I got a duck
in a pond surreal,
only floats around
in between meals.
Saved from a gun
plastic as he,
I got a duck in a pond I perceive.

Under a tree I went looking to find.
Caught a bird sunbathing, a preboarding pass.
Trail of a red-tailed hawk clears the mind.
I see rainbows at night.

Buzz in the hive,
I'm not alone.
Eyes open up,
feet know to run.
Bumble bee, humble me
please lead me home
where I can watch a duck
float in a pond.

## Adrift

Gentle angel, unwinged, human
flesh and blood songstress,
my song of seven,
gather this naked soul
fervent to the enchanted
touring the world,

esoteric feet
step where they walked before,
washed away never knowing
time, unlike prints on the moon.

We dig coquina clams.
Erudite sky and I
feel high, undertow,
each pull outward
flounder close,
creatures made of sand.

I swim to the edge of the world,
touch the center of the universe.
The way back is recurrent, a watery dream…

… a fragile effervescent rill
trickles and pours
vapors and rapids
requite to the core:
my gentle Angel,
ebullient heart -
a buoy.

## Conversation with Julio

Mystery-green '67 Malibu,
"My Girl" kisses
"Blowin' in the Wind…"
brains of teeth chomp
instigated men.

Errant hacky sacks,
South Mall's packed,
wish I had a dollar
for every participle ever dangled
over Littlefield Fountain -
all the tears we laughed.

Thoughts in hallowed halls
ricochet like super balls,
small clicks, countless doors
open and close Parlin Hall.
Twain, Shakespeare, Hemingway converse.
Julio, the eggroll/coffee tender and I
take the fast conversations in,
mock the madness walking by
radio, television and film.

Tippy toes in the fountain,
high-spirited blue eyes, more than
capable pretty woman
majoring in me.

"See you in the morning, Julio."
"Bien, bien, Mr. Bill," he says to me.
"Muy suerte," his whisper trails.

## Higher Ground

A dragon opens its eyes.
Heat lightning drives shotgun.
Windshield wipers, tears of heaven
cross the interstate,
mournful morning,
adjectives of lore.
Worn-out map
out the window.

The future is a highway,
miles of signs: today.
An exit says take me.
I make out echoes
around the bend.
Love evaporates from a distant pond….

Stones thrown high
touch eyes, mauve sky -
the sound of successful
splashdown.

## Phaedrus

Night owl slides
evening cries
horizon calculates
walking sunrise.
Phaedrus knows
all too well
Eros overflows.

Revolutionary life leaves a trail.
Rivulets meander, creeks crystal clear.
Rose sniffers see bottom, the world so small.
"I'm happy to be here." said the waking man
looking for diamonds, rough
cicada riffs.

Dialogue heats up.
Socratic instincts, self-preservation reserves.
Love is madness.  Time is
everyone's clause, rhetorical minds pause
four heavy horses….


She is making biscuits from scratch.
Laundry tumbles. Minutes crumble.
I stick around for another batch.

Smiling tells us where we are.

Neighborhood Walk
Lighthouse Watchman
All Happy
Vineyard Toast
Sides
Butterflies
Birdland
Achelous
Marathon
Twilight Man
Skeletons
Last Leaf
Recyclist
Cool Beans
One Night
Fable
Escape
Candles
Little Corners
Radio Waves
Spectrum
New Twilight

## Neighborhood Walk

Bats dodge.
Footballs fly.
Bonnets touch
azure sky.

Ears cock.
Cars allow.
Acorns bring
tinny sounds.

Two teeth weave
southern red sea.
Brown paths crawl:
Ant Hill Society.

Street's kickball.
Baseballs play catch.
Dogs watch tetherball.
Night, a lover, falls fast.

Door locks.
Blinds rappel.
Pigeon home,
exercised soul.

## Lighthouse Watchman

Kiwi birds know well the wind,
race the sand,
inhale its breath,
exhale second hands.
A clockface warbles
winter has broken.
All seasons hold true,
weather, unpretentious…


A lodestar sputters, flickers the pier
bare feet cross the dune, knife brackish air
fix the idle beacon,
hear ships' lonely call.

Salty pillar rusty,
beam stuck, empty stare.
Flare ups keep Pharos circling,
waiting for the glare
ascension into night.


My parrot tells me
when hands move
the distant dark no more minds the ambient
luminescent light of oceans
than unheard ticks of sundial mimes.

An exclamation mark punctuates the sky.

## All Happy

"C'mon in, he's in the back,"
my wife tells an old friend.
I take a break from the seed and handshake
ways of the world -
kids, wives, how lives survive
change.

We light bulbs of O'Keefe
smoke Whitman grass,
kiss Mother Earth
hug trees back -
our oaths complete.

Invisible hands
return from heaven, ajar,
a hot air balloon caught
writing on the wall, a stolen sky
eclipsing the sun.

Candide agrees
backyards suffice.
Happiness is a place anyone can go
get all happy,
covered in dusk.

## Vineyard Toast

Grapes in the veins,
long line of vines -
latest vintage from
a man of few words,
a mom of many.

Today is April,
Beaujolais.
Catching "It Had To Be You,"
wide eyes open brighter, Borealis blue,
more enticing than the half-light
tripping over the landscape

crossing an age-old wooden bridge,
the finish line of summertime.
The heart is a champion.
A couple from the sixties steps up
from the bank,
toasts their companionship:

Peace and war, toe to toe
never boring or lonely we go
longtime lovers, lifelong friends
forget the means, define the ends.

## Sides

Winter solstice stretches cold
bright blue breezes into brighter gold
clothespins and pastel sheets,
the homestead flank of the farm.
House whispers,
shouts from the barn.

Feet on solid ground,
hands twixt the push,
the pull of barbed wire
bounces the slack:
upright push-ups.

Finger to the wind
nose to the grind,
prairie home companions
stay on the side
every day growing
some kind of grain.

Come the morrow,
turned out, she'll see
storm cropped horizon
tightrope walking
the edge of a ledge, giant sunflowers
talking to a scarecrow
waving.

## Butterflies

Autumn somersaults
warm eastern breeze.
Leaves cartwheel
western trees
round my yard, north of town
top the brown
crouton ground:
a dressing.

My turn to rake
sanity's sake, pile high
the clumsy procession.

They fly away as I leave the ground.

## Birdland

Bird up
itchy branch
claws clench
righteousness.

Batman and Robin stop by
with Penguin to hear
Bird entertain
blackbirds and starlings,
color underwing.

Parker inspired
suspired in flight
bronze wings and fingers
woodshed heart:
moody, bluesy, groovy
*alto*gether apart -
feathers fly in the night.

The dizziness lingers.

## Achelous

Twilight drowns in a river
the moon bounces on
a trampoline it got
for Christmas.

All day words
leap like salmon,
coursing home
through a birthmark
on my cerebrum.

Untaken roads find the lyre's strum.
Ten thousand shadows cast down another one.
Rain leaves the forest, hear the dinosaur hum.
Trees borrow the wind, scratch naked winter.
Clouds slide off the sky.

My sleep walks, long
talks with the river god.
We discuss *The Shack,*
the earth explodes
lava blue; the gloaming descends,
the yin and yang of revolution.

## Marathon

Serious rain, Monday, same day.
First day of school.
Mothers grab their kids
boots, jackets and scramble
eggs, the sodden morning.
Baby birds hop to pilot school, chirping like the
children.
Wife's whistling to *Parkening Plays Bach*
wanting the rain to let up.
I return from the schools,
Pheidippides.

Some you lose, some you win.
Today only matters
if we wake up. And when
dreams bleed like love,
backs need a shove,
jumpstart shakedown
real-time truth:
the jig of the fiddle
the gig of the giggle
the jog of the jiggle
the tug from the toggle.

Roads run down,
sidewalks, un-hollow
drips on the pavement
we leave, we follow
world perfectly content,
chasing Apollo.

## Twilight Man

Twilight Man sees the crime,
the rise and fall of the sun,
fingers of light speak to the clouds,
lightning bugs rescue the moon.

Midnight parlays,
hidden stars bathe,
meteors shower today.
Unwashed cars, hill country bars,
winding river road parade.

Before anyone knows
twilight man paints the fence
chats, picketed, with Daybreak
nibbling a potato and egg taco.
Neighborhood talks coffee and pillars,
arbored ramadas.
The wind is not.

Down the street,
someone is picking guitar
softly, trusting whoever is up
with their strum.
In a house of light
dust plays offense,
pencil drawings wait their turn.

Earth returns half the sun
parched, other half, slaphappy.
Every phase of moon dances,
twilight man chants,
grail of orison spills -
the dense dry night.

Skeletons

Time levels the field,
bequeaths its depth
equally all around,
withered seasons whither
pecan and mesquite
rock unseen
under fading fern
until the cedar.

Planets chase their mood,
whisper satellite news.
Ghosts of constitution
bookmark each day.
Fridge quotes Voltaire.

Film we are, books under lights,
matinees by day, marquees at night,
favorite movies, shows and songs…
'til the next one comes along.


The hour is high,
a rumble is nigh
giving and taking
a roughshod ride.
Tumbling shells
bones we become
cheek by jowl,
skeletons of good lives.

### Last Leaf

Sad leaves
winter dissolves
night breathes, clouds
isolate, fade in the grey
wind and decay.
Leaves of family trees
never die, only far away:
fertilizer, I tell the kids.
Out back. Sunday.
They go back in.

Finches inhabit
deck light ceiling fan.
My id reads Roethke, superego, Cummings -
madmen for more
leaving only some know.

>

*Words for the Wind*
delicate pages turn
sensitive, deliberate souls -
clean, soiled,
burned.

Boxes of rain drain down
sheaths, trickle every blade,
each foot kicking in doors,
rooted homes, termites watch TV.

Heading in, I pick the dead out
the potted plants and walkways to my mind -
entrances only some know.

I retreat to a cave
I crave thinking
about time being
always in season,
Albert Goldbarth's "POETS CAN'T COPE" t-shirt
and the last leaf on a tree.

Recyclist
---------

Yesterday, I was a river
an ever-flowing stream,
peddling into a tributary
instincts geared for the sea.

Under the wheels of today rolls evaporation
thru valleys vast, deserts plain,
rises over mighty mountaintops
completes the cloudy chain.

Tomorrow the Earth continues spinning,
sun or rain steers every peak.
I'll be returning to a river
connects myself back to me.

Cool Beans

No moon.
Billion stars.
I remember a couple names.
I'm looking for one
named after her,
a birthday gift she got
when our souls met
before we were born.

Coleman and I hunt rabbit.
Whispers hike back, muttering field,
the bullet from Barney's gun.

Big Tree nightcaps the day,
hands to the blaze.
Midnight is perfectly unhazy,
stoked with the new moon.

Heaven is close enough to get a peek,
the code to her gate; Astraeus spilled the beans.
Milky Way hears me say
she's the coolest bean in the galaxy -
Elysian to me.

## One Night

Main stage waits
calendar proclaims
bountiful as Hades, beautiful as Odysseus.
The breeze changes
into its evening clothes.

One night a dream came to her,
she would be rich she said
showing off her pearl white shoes.
He was doing good work himself
tying up his own loose ends.
All four step out.
Uber (unlike Godot) shows.

Jet's Juke Joint.
Couples and then some
dance the night away.
Bold brass.
Boogie-woogie blues.
Big band jazz juice, justice
sweet sweat and golden.

Goodnight to the band, Amble,
cross the street, one vague headlight -
silent school park, empty zoo,
monkey talk in swings
(like social media) about everything
equating *Paradise Lost* to the day
the Armadillo World Headquarters was torn down.

A "Big Yellow Taxi" pulls up….

<u>Fable</u>

When no one's around
I cry and break down
for reasons why
I used to know.

The world's stopwatch revolves, Arthur resolves
to pull a sword from a stone
forged in Rome.
Brilliance is resilient.

Blackbirds murmur over powerlines,
Earth's thrum is clamorous.
Production works overtime,
construction is destruction.
Golden rule tossed overboard,
flotsam and jetsam, low tide stranded,
litter drying out, plenty
man-of-war.

Power is crazy, but unlazy.
Bones speak - again.
Mortality.
Recycle yourself,
leave yourself behind.
Morality.

A book of fables
falls off a drowsy bedside table.

Goodnight, Aesop.

<u>Escape</u>

Circus came to town.
Did not leave.
Second-hand command,
synchronicity.
Impatient patient steals away
the 5$^{th}$ floor, a self-made prison.
The only inmate becomes warden.

Close tape, rewind.
Open up, unwind.
Clocks reveal subpar, sublime.
Fast or slow, the TikTok of time
excites, delights
divulging. Memories prevail.
Some dim.
I remember stories -
a dog chasing its tail,
a shepherd crying wolf,
my brother walking away.

The world's off kilter.
Fingers accuse, points made.
Pirates raid the sea, invade the pond.
With all our telescopes, diagrams, scientific ingenuity,
empyrean curiosity, divine diversity…

"Can you tell me how to get,
how to get to Sesame Street
how to get to Sesame Street
how to get to Sesame Street
how to get to Sesame Street…."

## Candles

A spider I let live
weaves his sticky corner empire,
dew drooling in the lamplight
living for the spin.

Spinning is easy when it's 3:45.
Moon is sleeping, Night has no reply.
Power out, flashlight on the brink,
candles outside.

Sullen streetlights
lose their groupie, insect fog.
Tonearms lift from their groove.
Seconds tick away on a watch I do not wear.
Some say time marches on but the fool
on the hill tells me
time stands still.

A carousel spindle turns
candles flicker and glow
two ceiling fans churn,
smoke rings blow.

Silhouettes find a better place.

Little Corners

Talking walls sketch
ruins and glories of every nation.
Generations make their way.  Darwin sighs.

In little corners of the world
laptops and consoles sit -
dirty laundry, dinner
iPhones charging
innocence.

Trifles, trinkets, whatnots
beat-up radios,
boxes and drawers of every thought
I may or may not have honed.  Every debt I owe.

Up the stairs he wordlessly goes, knuckling the rail:
"Shave and a haircut,
two bits."

>

In a little corner of the world,
"Moonlight Mile" keeps the maple company,
its ensemble pebbles the window,
words on a puffy night breeze.
The jury is still, out
rehashing smoky flashbacks, cars unyielding.
Home is where I like to stay, pretending
I'm a Marquess, maybe an Earl.

In little corners of the world
nations cannot sleep,
caught in constant crossfire,
camouflaged commodities,
strangers calling home.

Attics exhale.
Broken basements, cold and weary
wash colors of every soul.
White lines on the highway, unclear and dreary,
long as a night can go…


Rush hour signals boggle.
Impatience revealed.
Love and money have us, tops in a whirl,
spinning to little corners
in our stunning, chaotic,
beautiful world.

Radio Waves

Radio on, "Yellow Submarine,"
dusty dials in, loud, unseen
memories stir distant chalet
tsunami-ed, lurking,
uncomfortable zone somewhere.


My horizon was christened eons ago.
Pirates on gale, dam let go.
Two sailor's charts
crocheted high seas -
the imparted glean, diffused fantasy.


Hands of salt, omniscient sea
susurration crescendos, you feel
everything.
Alone is never lonely.
Songs to be sung!
Wind sets sail for the sun. Artists know
night takes a stand.


She knows the poet inside her man
lowering the scope, sets no alarm.
Radio waves low, Calliope keeps score -
the slow-motion hop of sheep.

Spectrum

Glass interstice
sunshine not yet open
sweetness of Spring, sugar white magnolia -
sleep turns to stroll,
no city shadow.

The cock grasps
the hen came last,
God is the egg
Dawn cracks.

We rattle prattle and undertake
subconscious battles we like to make
intriguing conflicts, fortune and feign
cloudy interest in crazy and sane -
years of flash, tanks of gas, concert tickets
up in flame. Sun and Rain play colorful games.
"Now, then."

Strength of feet, coat of arms,
hands want to hold life's better parts.
Compass round, penpoints find
a ruse to rouse the rooster: Father Time.

Moon and Stars agree
Night and Day live between
wide-awake and sleepy dreams
spanning the globe, cliff diving:
"The thrill of victory, the agony of defeat,"
high school friends stealing time
time steals back.

I stroll back in.

## New Twilight

Outside right angles
left inside a compound
conjunction,
four not so square seasons
stretch chalk,
extend trapezoids into parallelograms
near my old school.
I drive thru neighborhoods
privy to my Treks,
grounds stomped thru
homes I recall
generations and the future
I ran into…

A weighty double pane glass door fairly slides.

Patio is cosmic, a teenager's bedroom,
someplace familiar, yet uncommon,
unique and exceptional,
a room in a house somebody else slept in
leaving a mannequin in the foray
surrounded by flowers and vine.

>

Truth and lies indeed thrive,
survive letters and words,
travel around the world.
Smiling life goes on
the bound; Road waves
derivation, despite its devices,
improvises the pot,
stirs the caldron hot
precise and contrived,
spontaneous and alive
voodoo.

The have and have not
obtusely reach out -
acute, somber edges see
two semi-circle schemes,
the sighted, the blind.


Rolling metal eyes
wooden arabesque
colorful marble spheres
quadrangle incense,
shapes of things here
end results there -
small clicks, big pics
mystery everywhere.
Time *can* be an ally.

>

Wind and Leaf dance
off the branch, no chance, no say.
Octagonal light slants
silver glass rectangles.
Locust scream over the eve.

Incredible is the time for a circle.
Cats are at play, mysterious castles.
The sky is a peach: necklace and ring.
A mother's smile is jewelry.


Light opens my box of fears,
its teeth and ears.
Coffee brews, a count begins -
all sizes and shades line and design
my engineered dream,
an all-colors-of-the-rainbow thing.

I live under the power of the sun,
sleep in the kingdom of Selene,
rise as Ben Franklin.
Pray for the dove,
chunk bananas to gorillas.
Sleep with the windows open.


Dryads in tie-dyes hold tomorrow up -
tiny transparent fingers, the gentle blue,
fancy colors.

There it is...

a new twilight.

"So we saunter toward the Holy Land; till one day the sun shall shine more brightly than ever he has done, shall perchance shine into our minds and hearts,

and light up our whole lives with a great awakening light, as warm and serene and golden as on a bankside in Autumn."

**Quotes and References (in order):**
Henry David Thoreau, Flannery O'Connor, John Keats,
Harry Nilsson (The Point), Robert Louis Stevenson,
John Bunyon, Smoky Robinson/Ronnie White, Bob Dylan,
Jim Murray, Gus Kahn, Garrison Keillor, William P. Young,
Christopher Parkening, Jim McKay, Theodore Roethke,
Judy Garland, John Milton, Joni Mitchell, Joe Raposo,
Milton Berle, Jagger/Richards, Henry David Thoreau

**Special thanks to:**
Angel Coggins – support and patience
Cody Coggins – production, New Twilight pic
Front and back cover, watercolors - author
Foreword by TR

Much, much love to Casey, Chelsea, and Christian.

Percentage of proceeds donated to the National Park Service.

Coggins was born in Greece.
He's lived in Virginia, Colorado and Austin, Texas.
an Antonio is his home now, where with his wife, Angel,
own and operate a custom screen-printing shop.
They have three boys and a girl.

printer by trade, poet at heart

www.ingramcontent.com/pod-product-compliance
Lightning Source LLC
Chambersburg PA
CBHW040741060526
44119CB00074B/191